# THE THROAT OF THE PEACOCK

## THE THROAT OF THE PEACOCK
A book of modern senryu poems on parents and children, with a sutra by the Buddha about filial devotion
translated from the Japanese and edited by
Harold J. Isaacson

Of the ways that lead to the high city, none is more fair than the road of filial devotion, but there has spread out a fog so obliterating all sight of it as to make one suppose that it is not there; although ever it lies infallibly tracing on, whatever may cause it to be overlooked. Moritake wrote: "In this world, those with filial devotion, such, whatever may befall, in everything remain steadfast." To take up such a subject is like picking up an angry cobra with bare hands; but the Buddha, that master snakecatcher, could do it, as in the beauteous sutra here translated.

Hardbound   ISBN 0-87830-158-5   W
Paperbound   ISBN   0-87830-557-2   W      $1.85

# THE THROAT OF THE PEACOCK

A book of modern *senryu* on parents and
children, with a sutra by the Buddha
about filial devotion.

Translated and Edited

by

Harold J. Isaacson

THE BHAISAJAGURU SERIES

The verses from Sankharacharya's *Devyaparadhakshamapana Stotra,*
translated by Arthur and Ellen Avalon in *Hymns to the Goddess,*
are used with the kind permission of the publishers,
Ganesh & Co. (Madras) Private Ltd.

The Bhaisajaguru Series takes its name from the
Sanskrit name of Yakushi Nyorai, the Buddha of Healing

The Bhaisajaguru Series is published by
Theatre Arts Books, 333 Sixth Avenue, New York 10014

*Dedicated to two Bills*
*Bill Pinckard and Bill Takagi*

# Contents

# PREFACE

Of all the splendid highways built from long ago that lead through many lands to the high city, none is more fair than the road of filial devotion. Reason for regret that in latter times, and in the more backward places, has spread out a Cimmerian fog of smutty vapor, such as described by Peacock in his *Melincourt* I think, so far obliterating all sight of this way as to make one suppose that it might not be there; although ever it lies infallibly tracing on, whatever deficiencies may cause it to be overlooked.

Moritake begins his hundred poems on *Yo no Naka* with :

> *Yo no naka no*
> *oya ni kō aru*
> *hito wa tada*
> *nani ni tsukete mo*
> *tanomoshiki kana*

"In this world, those with filial
devotion to parents, such, whatever
may befall, in everything remain
steadfast."

And this Moritake was the founder of a new form of poetry which became in succeeding ages the *haiku* and the *senryu*; then eventually, in process of debilitation, the new *haiku* and new *senryu*. So that it is very fitting at this late time to use the latest of the forms of a poetry founded, in a sense, upon filial devotion, to bring forward again for the present day this excellent matter.

*"Yo no naka"*-----"this world we are in." Herrick writes :

> "In this world (the Isle of Dreames)
>    While we sit by sorrowes streames,
>       Teares and terrors are our theames,
>                                                                  Reciting."

This poisonous snake which the enlightened perceive to be a straw rope; or otherwise, where straw rope proves to be a poisonous snake, in this world as it is now, to take up such a dangerous and difficult subject as filial devotion, is like picking up an angry cobra with bare hands; only the Buddha, that master snake-catcher, could do it, as in the beauteous Mahayana sutra here rendered into English.

As for the title given to this book, that royal bird the peacock, whose cry is so severe and sober, like the Buddha's utterance in this sutra; a bird that resembles the pheasant which catches snakes and which tenderly rears its young; the bird which in the Kadamba forest at night flits and couches among the flowering branches in that season when young women are apt to wander by night--- let it be that its voice is harsh like the sound of a *senryu*.

A wayside teahouse. With straw-rope hangings. The menu: country *sushi*--somewhat treacly; and soggy *udon* with a bit of fat or gristle on it for meat. The tea is tasteless; cigarette-ads are the pictures on the wall; and the waitress wears an imbecile grin. But the journey has been long, O Traveler, with no food since the early morning. What you order perhaps will not taste as it should, but with good appetite, as you eat you may say---"Not bad !"

Some tea ?

Harold J. Isaacson
At a mountain house in
Ehime Ken, Kuma Cho, 1965


*yo no naka* - the world we are in.

*haiku* - a form of comic poem in seventeen syllables.

*senryu* - another sort of comic poem in the same form.

*sushi* - cold rice flavored and pressed.

*udon* - a sort of noodles.

# THE BUDDHA DISCOURSES THE FATHER AND MOTHER GREAT KINDNESS SUTRA

Thus have I heard: -- One time the Buddha was at Raja-graha on the Gridhakuta Mountain accompanied by a throng of Bodhisattvas and Sravakas, when bhiksus, bhiksunis, upa-sakas, upasikas, dwellers from all the heavens, as well ac Nagas, Demon Gods and such, wishful to hear the Dharma, came together there. With singleness of heart they stood around the treasure seat, without the blink of an eye gazing upon the august countenance. At this time then, the Buddha deigned to discourse on the dharma and said, "All you excellent young men and excellent young women, in a father there is loving kindness, in a mother there is compassionate kindness. What is meant is that people born into this world have their karmic accumulation as the inner cause, and father and mother as the immediate causative factor of relationships.

"If it weren't for the father they wouldn't have life, if it weren't for the mother they couldn't be brought up. Or we may put it that they obtain their vital spirit from the father's seed and their form is shaped by the mother's womb. Because such is the inter-meshwork of causes that produces them, there is nothing in the world that can compare with the concern that the compassionate mother has for the child. Her kindness extends to even before there is a form. From the time that she first receives it in her womb, for a period of ten months continuously going, stopping, sitting, lying down, whatever she does, she receives all sorts of discomforts. As there is no time when these discomforts cease, the food and drink she usually enjoys, or the obtaining of fine clothes, or such thoughts as she is prone to find attractive, concern for none of these springs up. Just with all her heart what she thinks about is, if she can safely give birth to the child. When the months are completed and the days sufficient, and she reaches the time of bearing it, the wind of karma blows, it begins to be urgent in her, all of her bone joints ache, a fatty sweat pours from her, and her anguish is hard to endure. The father too, his heart and person alarmed and worried, has anxious thoughts for the mother and child. All the various relatives and connections too are anxious and concerned. When finally it is born and fallen onto the grass, the delight of the father and mother has no bounds. It is just like an impoverished woman who has obtained a wishing jewel. When the child first raises its voice, for the mother too, it is as if she had just been born into the world.

"Thereafter it makes the mother's bosom its sleeping place, it makes the mother's lap its playing place. It feeds from the mother's breasts; the mother's tenderness is very life to it. When it is hungry and wants food, if it weren't for the mother it wouldn't eat. When it is thirsty and wants what to drink, if it weren't for the mother it wouldn't drink.  When it is cold and wants additional garments, if it weren't for the mother it wouldn't be clothed.  When it is hot and wants to take off clothes, if it weren't for the mother it wouldn't get them off. Even when the mother herself is hungry, she takes what she has in her mouth and feeds her child with it; even when she feels the cold, she takes off what she is wearing and puts it on the child. If it weren't for the mother it couldn't be nourished ; if it weren't for the mother it couldn't be brought up; if it chances to get out of its crib, then from its ten finger-tips the child eats what is unclean.  When added up, people drink their mother's milk to the extent of 7,150 gallons.

"Father and mother's great kindness is like the sky which has no limit.  If the mother has something to do at some nearby place, whether it be to draw water, or else to make a fire, or else to use the mortar, or else to grind something, any of the various things she is busy with, on returning to the house, before she has reached it she thinks, 'Now my child, has he been crying in our house,...he must be longing for me,' and her bosom flutters, her heart is excited, her two breasts flow and she is hardly able to restrain herself.  Equally, when having gone out she returns home and the child in the distance sees his mother returning; if he is in his crib, then he moves his head and shows signs of interest.  If he is outside the crib, then crawling, he comes out to her and whimpering, makes toward his mother. The mother for the sake of her child hastens her footsteps, bends down, stretches out both her arms and brushes the dust from it. Putting her own mouth to the child's mouth she kisses it, and taking out her breasts she gives them to drink. At such times, the mother seeing the child feels glad, and the child seeing the mother is happy. The two feelings make one sphere. In all the realms of fondness, there is nothing that exceeds this.

"At the age of two he leaves his mother's arms and begins to walk. If it weren't for father he wouldn't know that fire burns one; if it weren't for mother he wouldn't know that knives cut fingers. At three he leaves the breasts and begins to eat food. If it weren't for his father he wouldn't know that poisonous things are harmful to life; if it weren't for his mother he wouldn't know that medicines are helpful in illness. When father and mother go out or go to visit people's houses, if they should get there something delicious or unusual to eat, for themselves they don't care about eating it. They put it in their pockets and bring it home, call the child to come and give it to him. If ten times they come back, right up to nine times he obtains something, and having obtained it, he is always rejoiced and laughs and eats it. If perchance one time he doesn't get anything, he makes himself cry, makes himself shriek, and he reproaches his father and blames his mother.

"But gradually he grows up and gets to have friends, and

the father gets him clothes and gets him sashes; the mother combs his hair and smooths his topknot. All of their own best clothes, they give to the child to wear, and they for their part wear the older clothes or torn garments. After that he seeks for a wife and marries a girl from somewhere, and turning from his father and mother, he holds them more at a distance, while the husband and wife get to be especially close to one another. In their private rooms, he takes pleasure in talking with his wife. As father and mother's years advance, their spirits grow old, and their strength declines, the only person they have to rely on is their son, the only person they have to turn to is his wife. But still in all, the husband and wife from morning until night, not even once come to inquire after them.

"Or in some cases the father dies before the mother, or the mother dies before the father; then all alone the one keeps to an empty room. It is just like some solitary guest who is putting up at a lodging house. There never is any kindly feeling, never any pleasure of agreeable conversation. Late in the night under the quilts they feel chilly, the five limbs cannot be at ease. How much the more if there be in the bedding many fleas and lice so that until dawn comes, not able to sleep, many times tossing and turning they murmur to themselves, 'Ah, what kind of bad karma did I have to have gotten such an unfilial child?'

"Then it may happen that when they call the son he will glare at them or scold them angrily, and so his wife too, and his children, seeing such a thing, also will be berating the parent, putting him to shame, and bend their heads down to hide their laughter. The wife unfilial and the children undutiful, husband and wife combine to commit what is among the five impardon- able offenses. Or else it may be again that suddenly they want to tell the parents about something, and they summon them to give them orders. They may call ten times; nine times not com- plied with, in the end they get angry and scold them and say, 'You've gotten too old; instead of lingering in the world, why don't you hurry up and die.' Father or mother hearing this, grievous thoughts choke up their breasts, bitter tears spring from their eyelids. Their eyes grow dim, their hearts grow dizzy. In anguish they cry out, 'Ah, when you were young, if it weren't for me, you could not have been brought up, but still when it comes to now, this is the way it is. Ah, the fact that I bore you, much better had it never happened.' If there is a child who from father and mother causes such words as these to arise, that child then, along with those words falling, will enter into the hell, preta, or animal realm. All of the Tathagatas, the Vajra Devas, the five mighty Rishi, these even would not be able to save or protect such a one. The greatness of obligation to father and mother is like the heaven which has no limit.

"Excellent young men and excellent young women, if I were to explain this in detail, in father and mother there are ten kinds of kindness achievement. What are the ten kinds ?

"1. Bearing in the womb, guarding and protecting kindness.

2. At the time of birth receiving anguish kindness.

3. At the child being born, forgetting all grief kindness.

4. Suckling at the breasts, bringing up and nourishing kindness.

5. Moving into the dry and taking the damp kindness.

6. Washing uncleanliness kindness.

7. Swallowing up the bitter and spitting out the sweet kindness.

8. For the child's sake doing bad karmic actions kindness.

9. When it has gone afar, think and remember kindness.

10. To the very end concerned and wish to help kindness.

"The greatness of father and mother's kindness is like the heaven which has no limit. Such kindness efficacy as this, how can it be requited. The Buddha now will put this into gathas and recite it.

"The compassionate mother, when the child is in her womb, for the space of ten months shares her blood and flesh with it. Her body feels very ailing but the child's body through this gets to be completed. When the months are fulfilled and the time has come, urged on by the karma wind, through all her body are severe pains, the bone joints seem to separate; her spirit, heart and mind are agitated. All of a sudden her whole body is as if ruined.

If it is safely born, then it is just as if she had been brought back to life again.  When she hears the child raise its first cry, it is as if she herself had been born.

When it was first born, the mother's face was like a flower, but as she nourishes the child for a number of years, her form gets emaciated.  Even on nights of damp frost or dawns of icy snow, she removes the child to a dry place and she herself lies in the wet place.  The child will defecate on her bosom or urinate on her clothes, but with her own hands she washes it clean and doesn't feel repugnance at the smelly filthiness of it.

When she takes food into her mouth she wants to give some of it to the child.  The bitter things she herself eats, and the sweet things she spits out for him.

If for the child there is something which it is essential to provide, she herself will do deeds of bad karma, and though she fall into bad gatis, still is pleased to do it.

If the child goes to a distance, until he comes back and she sees his face, whether going out or coming in she thinks of him; whether sleeping or awake she worries about him.

As long as she lives she is thinking of how her life can be of use to the child, and after she has died, she prays that she may still be able to protect the child.  Such kindness efficacy as this, how can it be requited.

And yet in growing up and becoming a man, to raise one's voice or feel annoyed, to go against the words of a father or to be impatient at the words of a mother ; or when one has taken a wife, to be rebellious to father and mother, that is the way of a person with no gratitude, just as to hate or despise brothers or sisters is the way of a person who is envious. When one's wife's relatives come to visit, bringing them into the hall and making a feast for them, bringing them into family rooms and animatedly talking to them ------ah, ah, human beings do everything upside down. People who should be cherished, instead kept at a distance; people who should be kept at a distance, instead made much of.

The great kindness of father and mother is like the sky which has no limit."

At this time Ananda rose from his seat, bared his right shoulder, and bending his knee, put his palms together and said to the Buddha, "Bhagavan, so great as this being the kindness of father and mother, we who are children that have left the household, how ought we requite it? Please explain in detail about that."

The Buddha declared, "You of the Maha-Sangha, listen well. In the matter of filial concern, between those who remain in the household and those who leave the household, there is no difference. When one goes out, if one obtains sweet fruits of the new season, then one should bring these back and offer them to father and mother. Father and mother will be glad to accept them, and even if they can't eat of them themselves, yet they will straightway send them round to the Three Treasures, and by this offering will tend to bring into being their Bodhi Citta.

"If father or mother should be ill, one should tenderly nurse them, not leaving their bedside. Nothing about it should be entrusted to others. At frequent times one should inquire how they feel and tenderly one should prepare gruel. The parent, when he sees the effort of the child, will very heartily eat the gruel, and the child, when he sees the parent eating, will humbly for his own part feel better. If for a while the parent sleeps, getting some rest, then listen to his breathing. When he wakes from sleep, inquire of a doctor and bring medicine. Day and night doing homage to the Three Treasures, pray that there might be a cure for the parent's illness. Ever fixed in mind the wish to requite kindness, even for a second, the child does not ignore it."

At that time Ananda further asked, "Bhagavan, the child who leaves the household, if he diligently does things in this way, has he requited the kindness of father and mother?"

The Buddha said, "No, not yet has he managed to requite the kindness of father and mother. Should the parents out of blind obstinacy have no regard for the Three Treasures, so that they inconsiderately do harm to things, or dishonestly steal things, or not acting properly, they indulge in licentiousness, or not being sincere they deceive people, or deficient in wisdom they are addicted to drink, the child then should firmly admonish them and try to get them to realize what it is they do. But if they still remain unresponsive and cannot be made to realize, then he should bring examples for them, show similar instances, explain the principles by which cause and effect act, and teach them the painful consequences that will come of it. But if still, through stubbornness, he cannot get them to correct themselves, with weeping and tears and sighs he should instruct them, and himself cease to drink and eat. However blindly obstinate the parents may be, yet as they become fearful lest the child might die, drawn along by their feelings of love and fondness, they will make a great effort and turn towards the Road. If the parents' feelings thus alter and they respect the Buddha's five regulations of conduct, that is, they have consideration and don't kill, they have honesty and don't steal, they have propriety and don't indulge in licentiousness, they have sincerity and don't deceive people, they have wisdom and don't get drunk, then, in such a household it will come about that the parents act with fond concern, the children act with filial devotion, the husband acts with correctness, the wife acts with virtue, the relatives are in harmony and are amicable, the servants are loyal and obedient. The six kinds of domestic animals on down to the insects and fishes, all of them respond to the softening kindness. All the Buddhas of the Ten Directions, the sky nagas, demon gods, princes who have the way, loyal and excellent ministers, from them on down to ordinary people in general, by all these they will be respected and esteemed. Violent and bad lords too, and flattering, cunning retainers, evil men and wicked women too, and the 1000 malignancies and myriad distortions too, against such excellence can do nothing.

"In brief then, for father and mother, that in the present life they may live calmly and quietly, and that in the next life they may be born in some excellent place where they can see a Buddha, hear the Dharma, and for long get free from the wheel of dukha, to do such as this is to begin to requite the kindness of father and mother."

The Buddha further to enforce his explanation declared: "You the Great Sangha, listen well. For the sake of father and mother exert all your heart's strength. Whatsoever you may have of delicious taste, beauteous sound, fine garments, carriages and carts, halls and rooms, with these serve them. But if father and mother, though through all their life they may have had more than ample of pleasures and enjoyments, still if they do not yet have faith in the Three Treasures, then you still are not acting with filial devotion. What should it be like? Having a considerate heart, to practise dana; having actions of propriety, to regulate one's person. With gentleness and easiness to endure shame, with vigorousness to pursue virtue, and immerse one's mind in the utter quietness. Although thusly one may with vigor exert one's spirit in studies, still perhaps for one time one gives way to carousing and gluttony, feasting; --bad mistakes abruptly seek out an opening and malignant forces may then obtain an opportunity. Then without any regret on his part for what he has obtained, they captivate his feelings, cause anger to arise in him, make idleness to increase in him, and the citta to get confused, the wisdom to grow dark, until at last they cause his actions to become equivalent to those of beasts. Maha-Sangha, from of old down to the present time, such causes as these have hastened on the destruction of persons, the ruin of families, the endangerment of princes, and all this not without the bringing of shame to parents. As matters are so, children must deeply be mindful and think through things to a far point. And thus the degree of filial care and its promptness is a question that they must know about. These are the things which make the requital for the kindness of father and mother."

Then Ananda wiping his tears, rose up from where he sat, and kneeling on one knee, putting his palms together, said: "Bhagavan, what name should be given to this sutra, and in what way should it be regarded?"

The Buddha told Ananda, "Ananda, this sutra should be called Father and Mother's Great Kindness. If there are any sentient beings who once read or repeat this sutra, thereby they suffice to requite the obligation for the milk suckled. If with all their hearts they hold the mind-thought of this sutra, or if they cause people to hold the mind-thought of it, then you must know that such a person well requites the kindness of father and mother, and in a whole lifetime, whatever there might be of the ten badnesses, the five great offenses, the heavy ill deeds belonging to the lower hell, all of these fade away and that one obtains to the supreme path."

At this time Brahma Deva, Indra, dwellers in all the heavens, everyone gathered there, hearing this explanation of the Dharma, each one of them brought into being the Bodhi Citta. Touching their five limbs to the earth they shed tears like rain, and coming forward they touched their heads to the Buddha's feet, and then withdrawing, each one of them for himself joyfully put it into practise.

# Senryu

講談社版・浮世絵美人画・役者絵2 「春信」夏祭り（世界救世教蔵）より
Summer Festival by Harunobu

Sigh of relief.

her shape, as the sleeve-cord

she loosens---mother.

Kakō

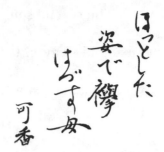

The true Japanese garment for women has long sleeves. When there is work to be done for which the sleeve would be a hindrance,  a cord is used to tie the sleeves up and back.   This is called *tasuki*.

Winter day.

In sleeve-strings mother

is still young.

Kōkeiji

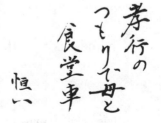

Filial action

in mind, with mother

to the dining-car.

Kōichi

The second son,

who made his way in the world,

takes mother on a trip.

                    Hōgetsu

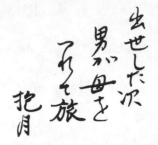


At come home drunk

father, the children

are delighted.

                    Shunsui

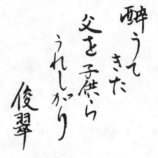


On this and that

treading, to be fondled

he comes to father.

                    Kaō

A boy child learning to walk.

After two children

the wife began to look like

a married woman.

                Kojorō

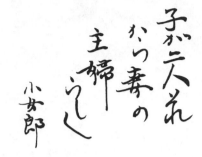

Western clothes,

getting out of them he

became the father of five.

                Gikonshi

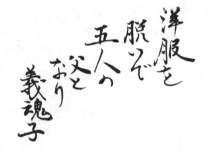

After the day's work, father returns and is glad to change into a kimono to relax and play with the children.

No-more-tears,

Father's standpoint

one day was reached.

                Suifu

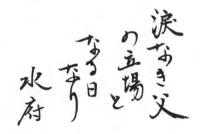

Among the crickets

all alone with

mother to live.

Gebunshi

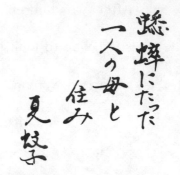

Perhaps a mother and daughter.

Lone mother

and daughter, amateurs, take

in boarders.

Bōjin

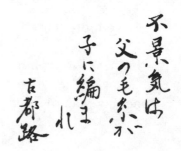

Hard times is

father's sweater-wool

reknitted for the boy.

Kotoro

Technical terms ;

after learning them, mother

was talked down.

Mokukei

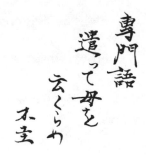

As she lies suckling the child

the wife's face in profile,

emaciated.

Gajin

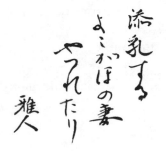

Father's fancy.

Son's fancy.   Goldfish.

Potted trees.

Teisen

The neighbor's

letter.  In it, something

about mother.

Sōsha

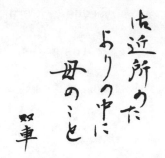

From both parents,

last night, words to make blood

run cold heard.

Sōsha

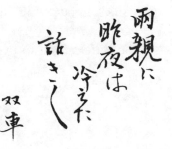

Father's tone of voice,

mother, with tears,

opinions given.

Takyō

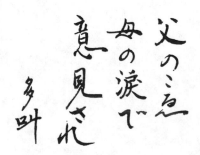

When uncle came

father's opinion

was bent round.

        Suisan

伯父がきて
父の意見
がまげられる
翠山

Make her worry?

Better to tell mother

    a lie.

        Shoshi

心配をさせ
まじ母に
嘘を云ふ
初子

The second son

who kept opposing

comes up in the world.

        Saiko

反抗を
つゞけた
次男出世
する
彩古

"Going to get

married," and fading away,

no more news.

Gorō

A tearful mother

there is--and that's what

our house is.

Hatō

Down mother's back

flows a towel,

much too big.

Kōfū

To send persimmons

to her son, the wooden box

mother herself hammered.

Reifū

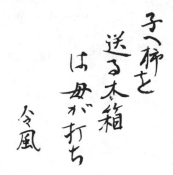

For a buttoned-jacket

father, they broil

a salt fish.

Kantō

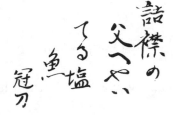

Father is a messenger, or an elevator operator or some such thing, and has come in for a meal in his uniform.

The children's candy

once in a while **becomes**

father's, mother's candy.

Sōnan

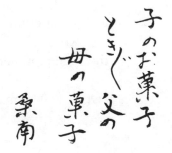

Faded coat

and things like that on,

to become a father.

Shunji

"This job is not much"

and while he was thinking that,

he became a father.

Senhan

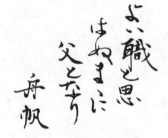

By the child

the face clutched.

Only 4 : 00 a.m.

Bijin

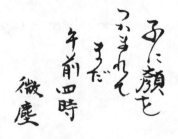

The dead mother,

in a dream her form just as

when she was young.

           Susumu

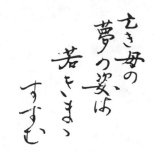

Mother

whenever she's alone,

a lost look.

           Jusanjo

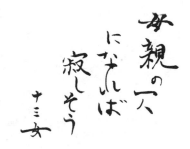

New Year's morning ;

even then by mother

awakened.

           Ikkyō

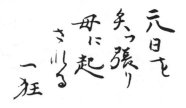

On New year's day people usually get up very early, before dawn, to pay respects at a shrine ; and so with this person.  Still just as on an ordinary day when he goes to work, on this day too mother has been up earlier and wakes him.

*Banzai ;*

among the crowd in tears,

mother.

Shōfū

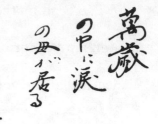

Banzai - "10,000 years", a shouting cry used in congratulatory and well-wishing circumstances, meaning "Cheers" or "Long Life".

Living apart, slowly

the wonderfulness of parents

begins to creep on.

Ninshō

His son's logic.

Nothing can be done about it;

to scold is forgotten.

Keirin

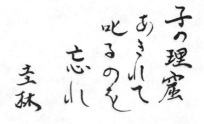

By the relatives

not to be outdone; ···what mother

is intent upon.

Reishi

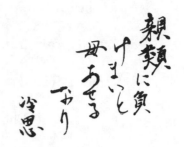

To no one

made known, mother's

deep sighing.

Eisen

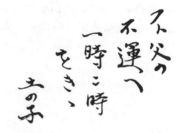

In father's sudden

disaster, one o'clock,

two o'clock heard.

Tsuchinoko

A sudden crisis has descended upon father and he is out to try to deal with it. The family waits up. One o'clock sounds, two o'clock sounds.

When it rains,

despite the rain, father

goes a-fishing.

           Chōko

雨ふれば
ふったで父は
釣にゆき
潮呼

Poem card meeting.

Mother's job only to

grill the rice cakes.

           Yoshio

カルタ會
母は餅やく
だけの役
よし緒

At New Year's the custom is to play *karuta,* a game made up of the Hundred Poems collected by Fujiwara Sadaie. The first half of the poem is read and the card with the matching second half must be taken up by the fastest person. That mother only grills the rice cakes suggests her aging.

On Mother's Day,

Mother's wish was just

        to sleep.

           Kanku

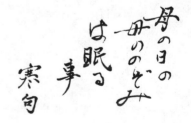

母の日の
母ののぞみ
は眠る事
寒句

School-girl.

To mother unintelligible,

her answer back.

Kōmu

For father

pouring wine, not a drop

should be spilt.

Bunkyū

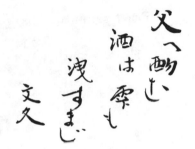

Hangover.

And a fond-of-scolding

father he's got.

Bonta

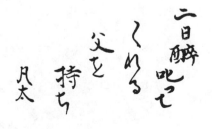

Hide-and-seek.

Mother in the clothes-rack's

shadow stands.

Shimei

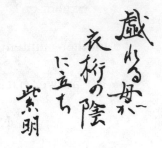

Practise on the bugle.

He has mother too

line up.

Senryō

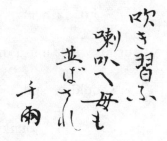

Filial devotion is

to stick on six cents to

the letter one writes.

Nikka

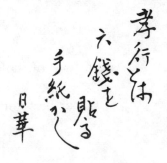

The son's sketch ;

father's moles

not unnoticed.

Kukō

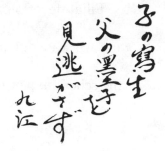

Of what he spends on *sake*

just a teeny bit is

what mother wants.

Zenshirō

*sake* - Japanese rice wine.

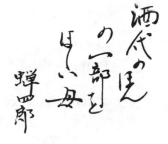

The voice that scolds,

at long last grows feeble ;

father's white hairs.

Rikō

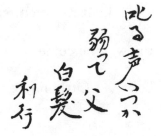

Filial devotion

is what we want for paying

the school expenses.

Biki

孝行を
してもらひ
たい学資
なり
美己

From the kitchen

mother too called,

good story.

Shōbi

台所の母も
呼ばれる
好い話
勝美

Like a reserved seat,

the way he comes to the lap.

Little boy.

Kaō

指定席
のやうに膝へ
くる男の
子
花王

To Father's

eyebrow movements

they sweetly demand.

Gajū

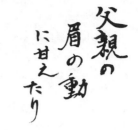

Though father wants to be stern with the children, they know he can be coaxed into giving them what they want.

If you let mother

speak, she'll say the children

are spoilt by father.

Tensei

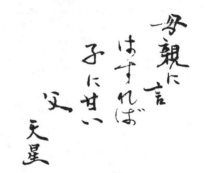

Towards a stupid child

the time and the season's

parental heart.

Roson

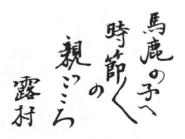

From eldest son

would rather live separately.

Father is young.

              Kamei

長男と
別居する
気の
父若し
佳鳴


As poor as ever,

now come to white hairs;

father.

              Junji

貧乏のままで
白髪の
父となり
淳兒


Return home.

A puzzle-ring brought

for father.

              Shinraku

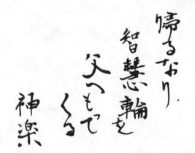

帰るなり
智慧輪を
父へもて
くる
神楽

Someone else wrote

the package label, but mother's

face floats up.

Seikandō

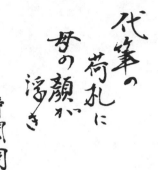

My determination.

Father's words made them

rounded.

Tensei

Even the way that

the shoe heels wear down;

like father, like son.

Hokki

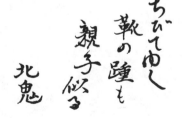

Father has

a big head too,

but my head !

            Ikkyō

Until the station

where there's change of trains,

mother uneasy.

            Hazumi

A Garden

magazine subscriber

father has become.

            Kasen

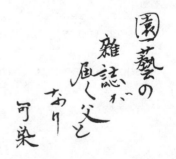

For the big sale

mother and daughter together

stand at the entrance.

Ki

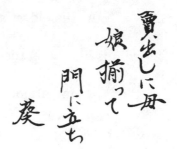

Her daughter's tennis shoes,

the trousered mother borrows

and puts on.

Seishō

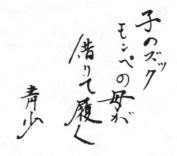

About the time when

she got to look like the dead mother,

taking care of hens.

Gorō

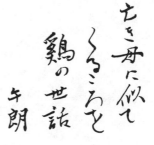

At the eldest son

who is like his father, mother

impatient.

          Fuchinshi

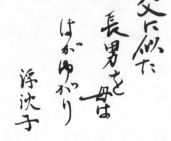

When it's a matter

of *giri,* father

puts on *hakama.*

          Sannanbō

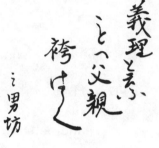

*giri* - The old Japanese ideal of acting with complete consideration for others and one's obligations to them.

*hakama* - the formal trousers of ancient ceremonial wear.

On the day

he wears a formal suit, by the children

looked up to.

          Kotō

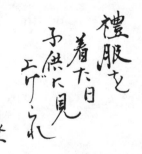

On New Year's

he doesn't want to scold,

father's face.

Goichi

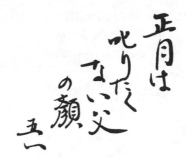

Mother's own

dishes have a home-

town flavor.

Shichō

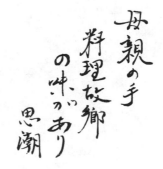

The maid usually does the cooking, but sometimes, for some special reason mother will make a dish.

Mother's way,

the bring-up-baby diary

in beautiful prose.

Shōta

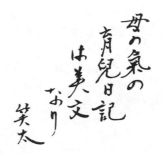

Unless you give him an ugly look

he won't do what he's told,

this child one brings up.

Nanten

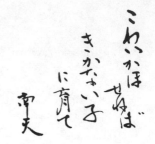

With dissipation

don't meddle, is mother's

advice.

Senjin

Through the cracks

blows the wind;  with mother

face to face.

Kōrō

*Donburi.*

With mother an intimate

night it becomes.

Gyōfū

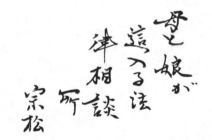

*donburi* - a one-dish meal.   A large bowl of rice with some fish or meat along
with egg and vegetable served on top of it.    This *senryu* describes a quiet eve-
ning at home.   Perhaps the *donburi* has been sent in from a neighborhood
restaurant, as is often done.

Mother and daughter

go into a legal

consultant's office.

Sōshō

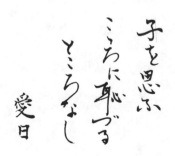

In a heart

that thinks of a child,

no shamefulness.

Aijitsu

Filial action

they let the radio do.

Young couple.

Ryūshū

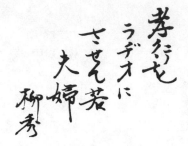

In the hymn

there's a part about

papa and mama.

Muro

Right to the bus

they saw her off,

the wife's mother.

Seiro

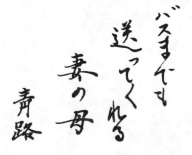

To father

who has a cold

a picture-book brought.

        Shinsui

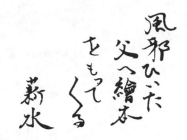

The child tries to bring what he thinks will interest father.

When the sickroom

calls her, with sleeve-strings

mother comes.

        Hisui

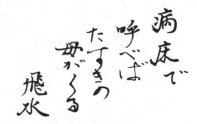

In father's

sickroom the things are

that the child wants.

        Kamei

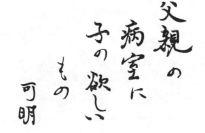

The towel

with the store name

mother uses.

Yoshio

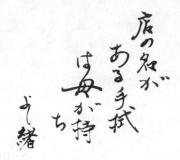

A towel distributed free as an advertisement.


Good fortunes'

mornings, towels but

no mother.

Sōba

Someone who has become rich ; in the meantime though, mother has died.


Like an *okimono*

the hibachi and father

are there.

Kōhei

*okimono* - a small statue or figurine group of wood, metal or ivory.

*hibachi* - a large container of ash wherein charcoal is burned ; a principal
apparatus for warmth in a Japanese room.  Perhaps the son comes home very
late to find father waiting up to have a talk with him.

On a beach-chair

in a bathing-suit, mother

gets young again.

Kizan

篭椅子の
浴衣の母は
若返り

奇山

Bamboo broom,

wherever it goes, in front of it

children flee.

Kotō

竹箒行く
さきくへ
子供逃げ

古燈

Father sweeping the garden perhaps.

For the filially devoted

child, a side-job at home

mother.

Hekirō

孝行の子
に内職
の母が
あり

碧朗

On maidenhood's

last day to walk with mother

shopping.

Bihō

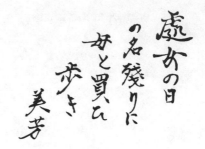

Of filial action,

not one jot accomplished,

she goes as a bride.

Muro

The crochet needle.

To a child crying outside

its attention divides.

Jūshi

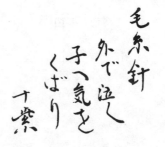

"No need for explanations !"

says mother with

gentle eyes.

Sentarō

One plum-bloom :

the thing that helps

mother calm down.

Bontei

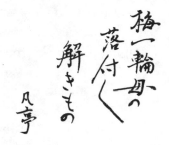

Just a father

and a son;  on the tray

scorched things.

Sansha

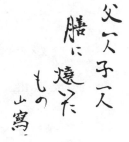

For further

filial devotion, money is

what's wanted.

Jūri

この上の孝行
金がほしい
なり
十季

What is strong is

night drinking father's

sweat.

Suifu

力強さは
晩酌の父
の汗
水府

To out-of-sorts

father, younger sister

the emissary

Harō

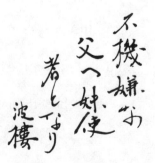

不機嫌な
父へ妹使
若となり
波楼

The go-to-school

child's hair, today

father combs.

          Kotō

登校の子
の髪今日
は父が
梳き

古燈


Plain and casual

relationship ; mother is

waiting.

          Seitō

淡白な
交際母が
待ってゐ
る

斉踏


Cash

enclosed, from mother

a letter comes.

          Kamei

現金を
入れて
母から便
くる

佳鳴

Mother still

wants to wait up for father---

arm pillow.

Kiku

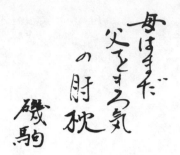

She rests her head on her arms.


For all our sakes

was the reason that mother

acquired a past.

Kinnu

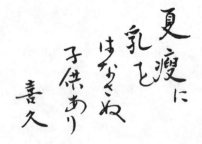


To the summer thin

belongs a child who won't let go

of her nipples.

Kikyū

His mother,

he provides for:

beret.

Kōmu

母親を
養うてゐる
ベレー帽
耕夢

When mother

stopped talking entirely,

that day's fearfulness.

Meishu

母親が無口
になった日
の怖さ
明珠、

Mother's tune,

one day without listening,

heard it.

Seika

母の唄、
或る日
聴ともなし
にきく
晴可

By another's brush

the scolding came.

Country mother.

          Bōsai

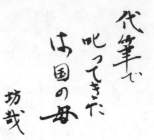

She can't write, so dictates her letter to someone.


Of the raise in pay

mother is informed;

night desk.

          Rensen

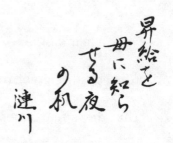

The young man has just gotten a raise.   He is back home in his room with some papers he has taken to work on at night, and pauses for a moment to tell mother about it.


To read while they walk

strictly forbidden, mother sends

them off in the morning.

          Nanka

Through this Spring

what is it that mother keeps

hinting at ?

Shisha

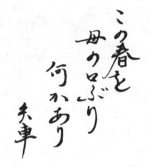

As I looked at the watermelon,

suddenly came floating

mother's face.

Aiko

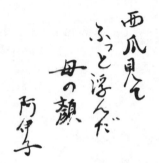

When according to the price-tag

it can't be bought,

takes mother along.

Seirō

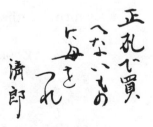

"Ask of your own

heart," said father and

went off to sleep.

               Yōgyo

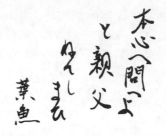

At the graduation

there was a lean-cheeked

mother.

               Ichirō

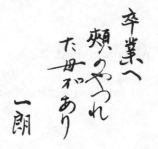

Night mosquito-net.

Just with one corner of it

wait for father.

               Chōnosuke

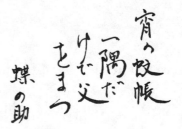

The Japanese mosquito-net is large, and often fills up the entire room.

Mother's

start of surprise:  on the second floor

was a woman.

Ushō

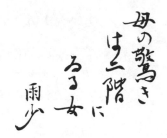

Lost his job.

On mother's lightness of

voice he lives.

Choshi

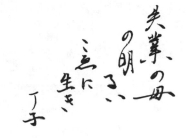

The moustache shaved off,

father, one moonlight night

was caught sight of.

Shōsaburō

Where filial action

is hard to perform--the metropolis,

lights shine.

Kansui

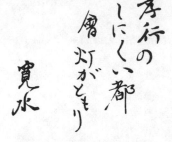

A good quality

Buddha altar is

mother's greed.

Jūshi

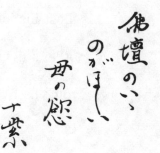

Father who always

wanted to go once to Manchuria,

has died.

Ninshō

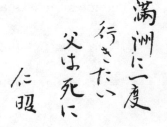

Pour for parent,

poured for by parent,

*sake* Autumn.

Teruo

親にさし
親にされん
酒の秋
てるを

Dependent on mother;

with a forlorn heart

he sweeps the garden.

Chiyoko

母に頼る
心淋しく
を掃く
千代子

Younger sister, whose

feelings were always artificial

has become a mother.

Shōkai

感情を
偽はる妹
母となり
章介

Electric *kotatsu*.

The cord frightens

mother.

Kajin

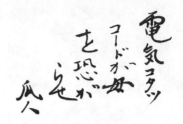

*kotatsu* - A wooden framework that a quilt is put over, in which one can sit or sleep in cold weather. Traditionally heated by charcoal, by now electric ones have taken over.

Borrowed money.

Father's greatness was

known that day.

Yūken

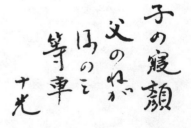

Child's sleep face,

father's sleep face,

third-class carriage.

Jūkō

Of filial action

one form:  meekly to

hold the umbrella.

Rikajo

孝行の一ツ
素直に
傘を
持ち
梨花女

Pitiless

eyebrows she lifts up,

village mother.

Kokushi

情ない眉
を見上
げる里の
母
国市

Father who

was hauled off by the police,

loved elections.

Kamei

警察へ
曳かれた
父の選
挙好き
可明

About opposition

to father---the operetta

was most enjoyable.

           Eisan

父親に叛し
歌劇の
おもしろし
映え

With new construction

wood scented:

mother's face.

           Kōga

新築の木
の香に匂ふ
母の顔
虎衛

For the second marriage

father's views

changed.

           Chiyoko

再縁へ父
の意見が
変るなり
千代子

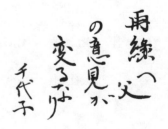

Father's seal,

as if it were a precious stone,

the way it's locked up.

Yashirō

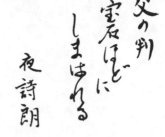

The seal is required to negotiate certain kinds of family legal or business papers. Perhaps the son wants to steal it for a few days to do something unknown to his parents.

In actuality

as ever, unfilialness

keeps on.

Seiki

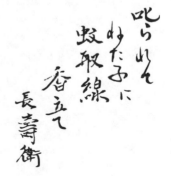

For the scolded and

went to sleep child,

mosquito punk put up.

Chōjue

# A HYMN TO THE DEVI

(Devyaparadhakshamapana Stotra)

by Sankharacharya

(vv 1–4)

## 1.

Alas ! I know not either thy *mantra* or *yantra,*

Nor how to welcome Thee,

Or how to meditate upon, nor words of prayer to Thee,

Nor do I know Thy *mudra,*

Or how to lay before Thee my griefs;

But this I know, O Mother !

That to follow Thee is to remove all my pains.

## 2.

By my ignorance of Thy commands,

By my poverty and sloth,

I had not the power to do that which I should have done,

Hence my omission to worship Thy feet.

But, O Mother ! Auspicious Deliverer of all,

All this should be forgiven me,

For a bad son may be born now and again, but a bad mother

there is not.

(Kuputtro jāyetā kvachidapi kumātā nabhavati)

### 3.

O Mother !  Thou hast many worthy sons on earth,

But I, your son, am of no worth;

Yet it is not meet that Thou should'st abandon me,

For a bad son may be born now and again, but a bad mother

there is not.


### 4.

O Mother of the world, O Mother !

I have not worshipped Thy feet,

Nor have I given abundant wealth to Thee;

Yet the affection which Thou bestowest on me is without

compare,

For a bad son may be born now and again, but a bad mother

there is not.


*mantra* - word sounds which embody an entity.

*yantra* - a diagram which embodies an entity.

*mudra* - a bodily motion or gesture, usually of the hands, which embodies an entity.

**DATE DUE**